Curriculum-Based Readers Theatre Scripts
Science

Rosalind M. Flynn

ISBN-13: 978-1463705480
ISBN-10: 1463705484

"Readers Theatre is a great learning tool. This is because you can have fun while learning at the same time. A lot of times, the stuff and facts you read from books go in one ear and out the other, but readers theatre really stays with you."

—*Eighth Grader*
Charles County Public Schools, Maryland

CONTENTS

ABOUT THE AUTHOR

 Rosalind Flynn has been developing Curriculum-Based Readers Theatre (CBRT) scripts with students and teachers throughout the United States since 1995. Over the years, she has learned a lot about what makes a CBRT script an effective tool for increasing retention of curriculum information, improving reading fluency, engaging students in a learning experience, and encouraging a theatrical delivery of the words on the page.

Rosalind focuses her work on the principles of arts integration. She has collaborated with students and teachers to create readers theatre scripts that integrate curriculum content and learning strategies with the skills and creativity of the art form of theatre. The CBRT scripts may be about topics that students would label "dull," but Rosalind gets students thinking like playwrights. They are writing to involve a large cast (the entire class) and to produce a script that entertains as well as informs. The results, which she shares in this and three other subject-specific books, are more than collections of scripts about facts that students need to know. They are dramatic teaching tools that involve students in reading, rehearsing, and performing. They provide students with the opportunity to practice speaking skills and stage presence, and to become kinesthetically and creatively involved in the theatrical delivery of a script. This script students practice and perform simultaneously reinforces the content information that they are responsible for learning.

In her book *Dramatizing the Content with Curriculum-Based Readers Theatre, Grades 6-12* (International Reading Association, 2007) and in her professional development workshops, Rosalind details the process of creating original scripts that address targeted curriculum objectives and information. Because she has led so many students and teachers in this work, she has hundreds of excellent CBRT scripts in her computer files. She took the best of those to create these script collections to share with educators who work with students of all ages.

Rosalind earned her PhD in Curriculum and Instruction at the University of Maryland. She is the head of the Master of Arts in Theatre Education at The Catholic University of America in Washington, DC. She is also a national teaching artist for the Education Department of The John F. Kennedy Center for the Performing Arts. Her e-mail is RMCFlynn@aol.com.

ACKNOWLEDGMENTS

The following is only a partial list of the playwrights and performers responsible for the Curriculum-Based Readers Theatre scripts in this four volume series:

At Westport Elementary, Springfield, MO: The students of Ms. Yielding

At Sullivan Middle School, Worcester, Massachusetts: The students of Mrs. Ryan

At Mosby Woods ES, Fairfax, VA: The students of Mrs. Gulino, Ms. Rohman, Ms. Carter, Ms. Bodenhofer, Mr. Tiller, Mr. Gray, Mr. Halvorsen, Mrs. Adams, and Mrs. Disantis

At Stanton ES, Washington, DC: The students of Ms. Walker, Ms. Riley, Ms. Kanes, and Mr. Spinner

At Blackburn ES, Manatee County, FL: The students of Ms. Seiderman

Project Stage Teachers, Manatee County, FL

At Desert Harbor ES, Peoria, AZ: The students of Mrs. Wilson and Mrs. Ulbrich

At Drew Model School, Arlington, VA: The students of Ms. Rohrs, Mrs. Lopatkiewicz, and Mrs. Labetti

At Lafayette Elementary School, Washington, DC: The students of Ms. Betz, Mr. Gregal, Mrs. Stanton, Ms. Brown, Ms. Breslin, Mr. Jewett, Mrs. Nickel, and Ms. Shapiro

At The Integrated Arts Academy, Burlington, VT: The students of Ms. Bonanni

Students at Sweet Apple Elementary School, Roswell, GA

At Kensington Parkwood Elementary School, Kensington, MD: The students of Mrs. Sandoval-White, Mrs. Boarman, Mrs. Architzel, and Mrs. Gehrenbeck, and Mrs. Howell

Mantua Elementary School students, Fairfax, VA

At General Smallwood Middle School, Charles County, MD: The students of Ms. Aravelo, Ms. Bell, Ms. Chastain, and Mr. Stark

At Mattawoman Middle School, Charles County, MD: The students of Mr. Wilson, Mr. Waddell, Ms. Wyman, and Ms. Scott

At Matthew Henson Middle School, Charles County, MD: The students of Ms. Gebhardt and Ms. Mouton

At Piccowaxen Middle School, Charles County, MD: The students of Ms. Pascarella

At Fort Hunt Elementary School, Fairfax, VA: The students of Ms. Enright and Ms. Blakeley

The Shelby County, TN Arts Infusion Teachers

Justine Crimans, Christopher Jarvis

Teachers in workshops, courses, and Summer Institutes at The John F. Kennedy Center for the Performing Arts in Washington, DC, The Peace Center for the Performing Arts, Greenville, SC, the Kravis Center, West Palm Beach, FL, Fruitville Elementary School, Sarasota, FL, Missouri Literacy through the Arts Institute, Lancaster, SC, and the Alabama Institute for Arts in Education, and Partners in the Arts in Richmond, VA

INTRODUCTION

What is Curriculum-Based Readers Theatre?
Curriculum-Based Readers Theatre (CBRT) incorporates the basics of traditional readers theatre—actors reading aloud from a script, performing without costumes, props, or stage movement (blocking). But instead of scripts that are based on stories or literature, CBRT scripts use school content areas as their topics—Science, Math, Social Studies, and English Language Arts topics, for example.

Each script in this book began as a list of content information—facts, ideas, and processes that students are supposed to learn. The nuts and bolts of how to develop CBRT scripts from lists of content information is the focus of *Dramatizing the Content With Curriculum-Based Readers Theatre, Grades 6-12*, published in 2007 by The International Reading Association. This book of Science CBRT scripts and three other subject-specific script collections (Social Studies, Math, and English Language Arts) serve as ready-made classroom tools and examples of scripts intended both to inform and entertain.

How are the scripts used in the classroom?
Speakers of the lines in the scripts are indicated simply by numerals on the left hand side of each column of dialogue. Numerals identify solo speakers, pairs, small groups, and whole group unison speakers—"All." Occasionally, to involve half the group in speaking, a script will read "Odds," meaning that readers with odd numbers read that line, and likewise for lines marked "Evens." Lines marked "Left," "Middle," or "Right" provide ways to have speakers with stage positions on the left, in the middle, or on the right of the group speak together.

Photocopy the scripts back-to-back (for ease in handling), distribute them to students, and assign speaking roles. It is helpful if students' lines—both the solo lines and those spoken with others— are highlighted in yellow. Then lead students through reading the scripts aloud. The CBRT scripts are intentionally short in length for practical use in busy classrooms. Students who read, re-read, repeat, and rehearse a CBRT script in preparation for performance tend to remember the information in the text.

[gesture]
When you come to the stage direction [gesture], work with the students to come up with a gesture that will help communicate something about the words they are speaking. Because students will be reading from the script as they perform it, direct them to hold their scripts in their left hands and create gestures that they can perform primarily with their right hands and arms.

[sound effect]

Do the same when you come to the stage direction [sound effect]. Explore sound effects (vocal sounds, finger snaps, thigh slaps, etc.) that will help communicate something about the particular words being spoken. Determine the best sound effect and use it in that portion of the script.

[X]

Some CBRT scripts contain a stage direction that is simply an X in brackets [X]. That stage direction occurs in chants to indicate a rest or a beat within the chant. Have students slap their thighs or snap their fingers on the beat when they see [X].

May the CBRT scripts be altered in any ways?

Absolutely!

Please feel free to alter or edit the scripts in any or all of the following ways:

Adjust the number of solo speakers—Add speakers if you have more students than the script accommodates, or revise the script so that there are fewer speakers.

Adjust the curriculum terminology—Change the script wording so that it accurately reflects your curriculum's terminology.

Change unfamiliar wording or expressions—Perhaps there's a phrase that's gone out of date or perhaps your students come up with an expression they'd prefer to use. Make edits during the initial readings and rehearsals and use your altered version of the script.

How are CBRT Rehearsals conducted?

Focus on one column of the script at a time.
Read through that column, make decisions about gestures and sound effects, practice the way that lines spoken by "All" will be delivered, encourage students to use vocal expression and characterization, and then read through that same column again (and possibly again) before moving to the next column. Approach each column in the same way and then rehearse the entire script.

Rehearse the script until the students are reading fluently.
Conduct the initial rehearsals with the students seated at their desks or standing behind them. The repeated reading of the same text increases students' reading fluency; the repetition of the script's content information contributes to their retention of the information. The gestures add a kinesthetic element to the reading activity. Students' projection and expression grow stronger in repeated rehearsals.

Assign "stage positions."

Once the students are familiar and fluent with the script's lines, gestures, and sound effects, assign them a position for performance. This position may simply be where they will stand in the semi-circle of their classmates when they enter another classroom to perform. It may be the step or riser they stand on for a performance in the school all-purpose room. You may choose to have half of your students seated in chairs while the other half stands behind them. Once students have their stage positions, rehearse the script with students in position.

Encourage the students to act with energy and expression!

During rehearsals, emphasize the importance of delivering the script as an energetic and entertaining piece of theatre. Coach students to speak loudly and with expression. Assure them that their audiences will appreciate a lively, well-prepared performance.

How important is it that the students perform the CBRT script?

The goal of performance is overwhelmingly motivating for most students. Working towards a performance is what makes students willing to read, re-read, and rehearse a CBRT script many times. For many students, it's one of the few opportunities they will ever have to present a rehearsed piece for an audience. For many students, it's as thrilling as a Broadway opening and they experience the same exciting jitters! The performance of the CBRT script transforms a reading experience into a theatrical experience.

The Layers of the Earth
Curriculum-Based Readers Theatre Script

1   Good morning, travelers!

2   Thank you for booking a tour with...

All   **Inner Core Travel!**
[gesture] [sound effect]

3   where our motto is...

All   **"We get to the core of things!"**
[gesture]

4   Today's destination is...

All   **The center of the Earth!**
[sound effect]

5   Yes—home of heavy metals. [gesture]
[sound effect]

6   Sit back, relax, and get ready to
explore...

All   **The four layers of the Earth:**
[gesture]

7   The Crust

All   **The Crust [gesture] [sound effect]**

8   The Mantle

All   **The Mantle [gesture] [sound effect]**

9   The Outer Core

All   **The Outer Core [gesture] [sound
effect]**

10   The Inner Core

All   **The Inner Core [gesture] [sound
effect]**

11   The deeper layers of the Earth are
composed of...

All   **heavier materials. [gesture] They're
hotter, denser, under much greater
pressure than...**

12   the outer layers...

All   **which are way cooler! [gesture]**

13   First stop—The crust!

All   **The layer that we live on.**
[gesture] [sound effect]

14   The crust is the most studied and
understood layer of the Earth.

All   **Made of the lightest materials—
basalts and granites
and rocks. [sound effect]
Basalts and granites and rocks, oh
my!**

15   How thick is it?

All   **The crust is between 3 and 25 miles
thick!**

15   Oh my! [gesture]

16   The crust is a thin, rocky skin.
[gesture]

All   **Thin, rocky skin. [gesture]**

17   The thinnest part of the crust is under
the ocean. [gesture]

All   **The crust [gesture] [sound effect] is
thinnest under the ocean. [gesture]
[sound effect]**

18   The ocean floor is heavy, dense rock.
[gesture] [sound effect]

All   **The ocean floor is heavy, dense rock.
[gesture] [sound effect]**

19   And the land is lighter, less dense
rock. [gesture] [sound effect]

All   **And the land is lighter, less dense
rock. [gesture] [sound effect]**

20   Traveling deeper into the Earth, we
arrive at the mantle.

1   The mantle is hot!

All   **The mantle is hot, hot, hot! [gesture]**

2   It's made of flowing asphalt.

3   You mean like blacktop?

4   Yeah, 1800 miles of it! [gesture]

 Developed by Rosalind M. Flynn ★ www.rosalindflynn.com

All	**Wow, that makes the mantle the largest, thickest layer of the Earth! [gesture]**
5	Hey, I hear there are two parts of the mantle: the upper part—
All	**It's cooler [gesture] [sound effect]...**
6	than the deep mantle, which is very hot!
All	**Hot, hot, hot! [gesture]**
7	Oh wow—we just moved—what happened?
8	The deep mantle rides on top of the hot outer core.
9	It causes the mantle and the crust to slowly move.
All	**Oh wow!**
10	Ladies and gentlemen, we have arrived at the outer core—
All	**Iron and nickel in the liquid state! [gesture]**
11	What?
All	**Extremely hot and fluid! [gesture]**
12	Fiery and furiously hot and fluid!
13	How dense is the outer core?
All	**Fourteen hundred miles thick! [gesture][sound effect]**
15	We are approaching our final destination—the inner core!
16	The inner core—nickel and iron in the solid state,
17	800 miles thick—
All	**Inner core! Inner core! [gesture]**
18	What is it made of?
All	**Nickel and iron, nickel and iron—solid! Solid—solid as a rock! [gesture]**
19	That concludes today's journey through the layers of the Earth.
2	Thank you for booking a tour with...
All	**Inner Core Travel! [gesture] [sound effect]**
3	where our motto is...
All	**"We get to the core of things!" [gesture]**

Renewable Energy Sources
Curriculum-Based Readers Theatre Script

1 And now for a message from our sponsor...

2 Are you going into debt from your energy bills?

3 Are you worried about the environment?

4 Are you wondering...

5 There must be alternative energy sources! [sound effect]

4 Then you're ready for...

All **R.E.S.! Renewable Energy Sources! [gesture] [sound effect]**

6 Gee, mister! I want to learn about that!

7 Do tell. What are renewable energy sources?

All **Renewable energy comes from sources that can be naturally replaced. [gesture]**

6 Radical! I don't get it.

8 And—R.E.S. does not come in one form—

9 R.E.S. comes in Six Different Forms!

All **Solar Power [gesture]**

Hydropower [gesture]

Biomass [gesture]

Geothermal [gesture]

Wind Power [gesture]

And Tidal Power [gesture]

10 What in tarnation?!

11 I really have no idea what any of those are!

12 I do! Renewable energy sources...

All **harness natural powers. [gesture]**

13 Harness? Like a horse or a pony? [sound effect] [gesture]

All **[sound effect] [gesture]**

No! Harnessing means harvesting or converting power.

14 Well, there are 6 forms. Which one is best for me and my family?

15 It depends on where you live!

16 If you live where it is sunny most of the time, what's best for you is...

All **Solar Power! [gesture]**

17 Solar power converts sunlight to heat and electricity.

18 If you live near a large river, the best renewable energy source for you is...

All **Hydropower! [gesture] [sound effect]**

19 Build yourself a dam or a water wheel and use the power of flowing water to make electricity!

20 "Build Your Own Dam Kit" sold separately.

21 Batteries not included. Adult assembly required.

22 If you live near a farm, the energy source for you is...

All **Biomass! [gesture]**

22 Biomass the process of burning plant or animal waste or products for energy.

23 Mmmm. Biomass. I like the sound of that!

24 If you make your home near a volcano,

25 geyser,

26 or anywhere around the Ring of Fire,

27 Then you need...

All	Geothermal! [sound effect] [gesture]
1	What is geothermal?
24	Geothermal energy captures heat from the earth's core.
25	Like, OMG, that's HOT!
2	Do you live in a normally windy area?
3	If you do then it would be prudent to invest in...
All	**Wind Power! [sound effect] [gesture]**
4	Wind power takes the wind and rotates a turbine.
5	The mechanical energy from the wind is converted into electricity.
6	You're confusing me!
7	Well, what this really means is that the wind moves the turbine or windmill and takes the power to houses and buildings.
6	Oh now I get it!
8	If you live near an ocean, your best renewable energy source is...
All	**Tidal Power! [sound effect] [gesture]**
9	Tidal Power is generated by the incoming and outgoing tides.
All	**Surf's up, Dude! [sound effect] [gesture]**

10	Order now and we will upgrade your R.E.S. to...
All	**Platinum Version!**
11	If you want your children...
12	and your grandchildren...
13	and your great grandchildren...
14	and great great grandchildren...
15	and great great great grandchildren...
16	We get the idea! [gesture]
17	Anyway, if you want your descendants—
18	all of your descendants—
19	to experience the great world we live in...
All	**Buy R.E.S now! [gesture]**
20	Now!
21	We mean right now!
22	Call 1-800-R.E.S–NOW!
23	And Solar Power, Hydropower,
24	Tidal Power, Geothermal,
25	Biomass, and Wind Power can be all yours!
All	**R.E.S. Buy it now! [gesture]**

The Water Cycle
Curriculum-Based Readers Theatre Script
(*or* Molly Cule and the Water Cycle: A Fairy Tale)

1   Once upon a time...

All   [sound effect]

2   There was a little drop of water named Molly Cule.

All   [sound effect]

3   Molly Cule lived in the Cool Condensation Castle in the Clouds.

All   [sound effect] [gesture]

4   She lived with a whole village of her drippy friends.

All   [sound effect] [gesture]

5   One day, Molly Cule and her friends were very cold.

All   **Brrrr!** [gesture]

6   They all clung to each other causing...

All   [gesture] **CONDENSATION!**

1   They got very heavy.

2   The doors to the castle flung open.

3   And all the little droplet friends...

4   tumbled out of the cloud.

All   [gesture] **PRECIPITATION!**

5   They went down,

1   down,

2   down.

All   **Splash!** [gesture]

3   Into a stream they rained.

All   **Rained!** [sound effect] [gesture]

4   They rolled from a stream to a river.

All   **River!** [sound effect] [gesture]

5   From a river to a bay.

All   **Bay!** [sound effect] [gesture]

6   From a bay to the ocean.

All   **Ocean!** [sound effect] [gesture]

1   The sun beat down on Molly Cule and her drippy friends.

All   [gesture] [sound effect]

2   They felt dizzy and light-headed!

All   [gesture] [sound effect]

3   All of a sudden, they started floating up into the sky.

All   [gesture] [sound effect]

4   Like a gas!

5   In the air!

All   [gesture] **EVAPORATION!**

6   When they got way up in the air,

All   **they floated around and around.** [gesture]

1   Before they knew it,

2   they were all back in the Cool Condensation Castle in the Clouds.

All   [gesture] [sound effect] [Look around at one another in recognition.]

At least for a little while!

The Water Cycle
Curriculum-Based Readers Theatre Script

1 3, 2, 1… We are live from Water Drop News. Today we have several guests from the water cycle. First up—

All **Aqua Daddy! [sound effect] [gesture]**

2 Who's your daddy?

All **You are. [gesture]**

2 I would like to introduce my four darling daughters.

3 Hi, I'm Condensation.

All **She holds water. [gesture]**

4 Hi, I'm Precipitation.

All **She really gushes on a rainy day. [sound effect]**

5 Hi, I'm Run-off.

All **We never know where she's going and flowing. [gesture]**

6 Hi, I'm Evaporation.

All **She's always disappearing. [gesture] [sound effect]**

2 Condensation, I thought you said you were going on a diet. You keep getting bigger and bigger.

3 But Daddy, I am not eating that much! I think it is water weight gain. I feel so bloated. If I could just get rid of some of this water…

All **How you gonna lose it? [gesture]**

3 I don't know.

4 I'm Precipitation and I know. Rain, hail, sleet, or snow. That's how you're going to lose it.

3 Oh, now I know.

All **We've been through rain, hail, sleet, and snow; Now sister Run-Off, where you gonna go?**

5 I'm on the lakes. I'm on the streams. I'm underground. I make the scenes!

All **Where you going now? [gesture]**

5 I could go up with the plants, or out to the sea—there are lots of choices for little old me. I think I'll choose Hawaii; I need to go for a swim.

All **[Hum a Hawaiian-like melody.]**

4 Is another one of our sisters here?

6 Guess who?! [gesture]

5 Condensation?

6 No, no, no!

3 Precipitation?

6 No, no, no!

2 Evaporation?

6 Yes it's me—Evaporation!

All **Hey-ey! [gesture]**

2 We should have known it was you when we couldn't see you!

6 Hawaii's been fun, but I can't stay. Sun and heat make it hard to play!

5, 6 Time to go see Sister Condensation.

1 Well Aqua Daddy, that's quite a family you have there.

2 I never know where they are. They all move around from near to far.

1 There you have it folks. You have heard from the Water Cycle family—

2 Aqua Daddy and his lovely daughters—

All **Condensation, Precipitation, Run-off, and Evaporation! [gesture]**

1 This has been Water Drop News—going with the flow!

Parts of a Plant
Curriculum-Based Readers Theatre Script

All **(Sing) Daisy, Daisy, give me your answers true.**

1 Attention all green thumbs and gardeners!

2 All florists and foresters!

3 Is the bloom off your rose?

4 Has your flower lost its power?

5 Then call...

All **Daisy Dioxide and the Green Team! [sound effect] [gesture]**

1 - 5 Daisy and team will...

All **get to the root of all your plant problems! [sound effect]**

6 Hiya Folks! I'm Daisy Dioxide. I know everything from root tip to petal about plants and I am here to...

All **help your garden grow! [gesture] [sound effect]**

7 Daisy! Daisy! My neighbor and I want to eat the green beans we planted, but they are way too small.

8 What do we feed them so that they can feed us?

6 What have you tried to feed them so far?

7, 8 A hamburger, curly fries, and Diet Coke.

All **Oh no! [sound effect] [gesture]**

6 Plants need a special diet that is much different from what you and I eat.

All **Plants use photosynthesis to eat.**

7 Photo what?

1 Don't you know what photosynthesis is?

8 Is that when everyone's smiling in the picture? Everybody say, "Cheese!"

All **Cheese!**

6 No, No! Photosynthesis is a process that plants use.

All **Photosynthesis is the process that plants use to make their own food.**

7, 8 How does photosynthesis work?

2 The leaves of a plant catch the sunlight and then turn it into sugar.

Evens (Sing) Oh Mister Sun, Sun, Mister Golden Sun. [gesture]

Odds (Sing) Please shine down on leaves. [gesture]

3 The leaves also...

All **inhale carbon dioxide. [sound effect] and exhale oxygen. [sound effect]**

9 Hey! That's the opposite of what people do!

10 Exactly. Plants breathe carbon dioxide, but people and animals breathe oxygen.

6 So find your green beans a nice sunny spot in your garden, skip the curly fries, and give them plenty of air. They'll be well fed and soon you will be too!

11 Daisy! Daisy! What will my petunias look like when they grow up?

6 Just remember a flower has a body a lot like you do! A head...[gesture]

All **The flower!**

4 Shoulders...[gesture]

All **The stem!**

5 Knees...[gesture]

All **The leaves!**

1 And toes. [gesture]

All **The roots!**

6	Sing it, Green Team!

All **Flower, stems, and leaves and roots, leaves and roots. [gesture]**
Flower, stems, and leaves and roots, leaves and roots. [gesture]

6   So remember, even though your petunias start out as little seeds, they can all grow big and strong.

11   How?

12   First the leaves catch the rays of the sun...

All **and the carbon dioxide from the air. [gesture]**

13   Then the stem, which is full of little tubes, goes to work.

All **The stem holds the plant *above* the ground and carries sugar from the roots to the petals of the flower. [gesture]**

14   The roots soak up water and nutrients from the ground and store them for later.

All **The roots hold the plant *in* the ground and soak up water and nutrients. [sound effect]**

6   But most importantly... the flower (or the petal) creates seeds.

All **The flower—attracts insects [sound effect] and creates seeds!**

11   Why is that most important?

1   So that one flower...

1, 2   can create another flower...

1 - 4   which creates more flowers...

1 - 14   which create bunches of flowers.

All **That makes a big, beautiful garden! [gesture] [sound effect]**

15   Daisy! Daisy! I've always heard that it's not easy being green. Then why are so many plants green?

6   Plants are green because of chlorophyll.

All **Chlorophyll is a green pigment found in the leaves of plants.**

16   And that chlorophyll is mighty important because it helps in...

All **Photosynthesis! [gesture]**

6   That's all for today, folks. I've got to get back to my garden! This is Daisy Dioxide...

1 - 5   and the Green Team helping you to...

All **get to the root of all your plant problems! [gesture]**

17   See you next time!

All **Flower, stems, and leaves and roots, leaves and roots. [gesture]**
Flower, stems, and leaves and roots, leaves and roots. [gesture]

Ecosystems
Curriculum-Based Readers Theatre Script

1 And now for a message from our sponsor—

All Biome-matic Travel! [gesture] [sound effect]

2 where our motto is...

All "We are eco-systematically correct!" [gesture] [sound effect]

3 We think you need to tour...

All every ecosystem on earth! [gesture]

4 What's an ecosystem?

All An ecosystem consists of all the plants and animals found in a particular location.

5 But wait! There's more!

6 Scientists group ecosystems into categories called...

All Biomes! [gesture] [sound effect] "Biome-matic Travel!" [sound effect]

7 We offer you and your family exclusive excursions to the Earth's six biomes—

All [Snap 4 times—X X X X—to begin a rhythmic chant.]

Tundra [X] [X] Desert [X] [X] Grasslands [X] [X] Forests: [X] [X] Tropical Rain, [X] [X] Deciduous [X] [X] and Con-i-fer-ous!

8 Tired of hot, sweaty summers?

All Then travel to the Tundra! [gesture]

9 ..where there are long, cold winters...

All [sound effect]

10 and even the summers are short and cool. [gesture]

11 Think it's too cold for you?

12 Well, it's not too cold for...

All seals, polar bears, foxes, arctic hares.

12 They have made the Tundra biome their home.

All "Biome-matic Travel!" [gesture] [sound effect]

13 They've survived through adaptation—

14 like white fur that blends in with the snow!

15 Do you want to thaw out?

All Then visit our next biome—the Desert!

16 But make sure you bring plenty of water because deserts are...

All dry and hot! [gesture] [sound effect]

17 What will we see in the desert?

1 - 5 Cactus,

1 - 10 camels,

All and varieties of frogs. [sound effect]

18 But how do they survive in such a dry biome?

19 They have adapted to surviving on little water by...

All storing water within their bodies. [sound effect]

20 Hey! Is that an oasis or a mirage?

All [gesture—All look in same direction.] No! It's the grasslands!

21 Yes, for a limited time only, if you take our desert tour, we offer a three-day excursion to a...

All "Vast Grassland Biome!" [sound effect]

22 How vast is the grassland biome?

23	On your three-day experience, you will explore millions of square miles of...
All	**sparse trees and extensive grasses. [gesture] [sound effect]**
5	But wait! There's more!
24	You and your loved ones will also encounter some of the largest land animals on earth!
1-5	American bison,
1-10	elephants,
1-15	and giraffes!
All	**Act fast, so you don't miss out on the experience of a lifetime!**
1	Next biome—the tropical rainforest!
All	**[sound effect]**
2	Precipitation defines this biome.
3	Look to your left. *{Pause for All to look left.}* You'll see an abundance of life forms:
All	**Trees, plants, ferns...**
4	And over to the right. *{Pause for All to look right.}* You'll see:
All	**Insects, spiders, snakes, and monkeys! [gesture] [sound effect]**
5	Take a deep breath.
All	**[sound effect]**
5	The tropical rainforest helps to replenish the atmosphere's oxygen supply.
All	**Without the tropical rainforest, our health could be compromised! [gesture] [sound effect]**
6	Now, put up your umbrellas. Let's keep moving!
7	The next biome on our tour is the deciduous forest with its...
All	**moderate precipitation [sound effect] and temperatures. [gesture]**

8	This biome is characterized by...
All	**long warm summers [gesture]**
9	and
All	**short cool winters. [gesture]**
10	and
All	**an abundance of deciduous trees!**
11	What's a deciduous tree?
All	**In autumn, deciduous trees lose all their leaves. [gesture]**
12	The animals in this biome include...
All	**insects and birds and deer—oh my!**
13	Travel close to either of the earth's poles to reach the next biome...
14	Fresh forest air,
All	**[gesture] [sound effect]**
15	high mountaintops,
16	short summers,
17	and long, cold winters!
All	**[gesture] [sound effect]**
18	See wildlife and get in touch with nature when the biome you visit is...
All	**The coniferous forest!**
19	Wow! There are so many biomes!
20	Where will we go first?
3	How about the d...d...d...
All	**Deciduous?**
4	Yeah, it's a biome with long, warm summers and short, cool winters!
5	Another happy customer who will tour the earth with...
All	**Biome-matic Travel! [gesture] [sound effect]**
2	where our motto is...
All	**"We are eco-systematically correct!" [gesture] [sound effect]**

The Rock Cycle
Curriculum-Based Readers Theatre Script

1   And now for—

All   **The Rock Cycle! [gesture] [sound effect]**

1   The earth's rock cycle begins with...

All   **magma... [sound effect] [gesture]**

1   beneath the surface of the earth.

2   What's magma? [sound effect] [gesture]

All   **Magma is hot molten rock. [gesture]**

3   That means rock in liquid form.

1   When magma cools,

All   **[sound effect]**

1   it becomes...

All   **Igneous rock. [sound effect] [gesture]**

2   Igneous?

All   **Also known as granite.**

1   Wind...

All   **[sound effect]**

1   and water...

All   **[sound effect]**

1   break the rock down into...

All   **sediment.**

3   Rock that forms from this sediment is...

All   **sedimentary rock. [sound effect] [gesture]**

2   Sedi-what?

All   **Sedimentary [sound effect] [gesture] or—sandstone.**

2   Oh.

1   If either sedimentary or igneous rock is put under a lot of pressure,

All   **[sound effect] [gesture]**

3   and heat,

All   **[sound effect] [gesture]**

1   these rocks change into...

All   **Metamorphic [sound effect] [gesture] rock.**

2   Metamorphic?

All   **Right! [gesture]**

3   Also known as...

All   **slate.**

2   So let me get this straight. Rocks are classified as either...

All   **igneous,**
[sound effect] [gesture]
sedimentary,
[sound effect] [gesture]
or metamorphic.
[sound effect][gesture].

2   One more time!

All   **igneous,**
[sound effect] [gesture]
sedimentary,
[sound effect] [gesture]
or metamorphic.
[sound effect][gesture].

Fossils
Curriculum-Based Readers Theatre Script

1   Up next on Discovery Channel—

All   <u>**Fossil Finders!**</u> **[sound effect – Theme music]**

2   Our guests tonight are paleontologists from...

All   **The National Science Museum. [gesture]**

3   What's a paleontologist?

All   **A paleontologist is a scientist who studies fossils. [gesture] [sound effect]**

4   What's a fossil?

5   Fossils are remains of plants and animals...

All   **that lived millions of years ago. [gesture]**

All   **[Chant]**

Fish,	**Teeth,**	**Dinosaurs,**
Bones,	**Eggs,**	**Arthropods,**
Leaves,	**Plants,**	**Insects, and**
Nests	**[X]**	**[X] [X] [X]**
Fossils!	**[gesture]**	

6   But why would we study dusty old fossils?

7   Fossils give us clues about life...

All   **millions of years ago. [gesture]**

8   I wish I could have a dinosaur for a pet.

Left Half of Group	**No way!**
Right Half of Group	**Not a chance!**
Left Half of Group	**That's insane!**
Right Half of Group	**Are you crazy?**

8   Why couldn't I?

All   **Dinosaurs and people NEVER lived at the same time! [gesture]**

9   Where do you even find fossils? [gesture]

10   Fossils are usually formed in...

All   **sedimentary rock. [gesture] [sound effect]**

11   Why?

All   **Dead animals got trapped and buried in layers of silt and mud. [gesture]**

11   Oh, I get it now.

12   Can you find fossils anywhere else?

13   Fossils are not often found in igneous or metamorphic rock because...

ALL   **...heat and pressure can destroy fossils. [gesture] [sound effect]**

14   How long does it take for a fossil to form?

All   **It takes millions of years for fossils to form.**

14   Really?

All   **Yes, millions of years! [gesture]**

14   Wow! That's a long time!

15   What else can you tell us about fossils?

BOYS   Tell me more! Tell me more! [sound effect – Think "Summer Lovin' " from *Grease*]

16   Like how many are there? [gesture]

All   **There are three types of fossils: [gesture]**

Left	Imprints... [gesture]
Center	and casts... [gesture]
Right	and molds. [gesture]

All   **Imprints and casts and molds—Oh my! Imprints and casts and molds—Oh my! [gesture]**

2   What's the difference?

Left	Imprints are molds of leaves or other thin objects.
Center	A cast is made when mud or minerals fill a mold.
Right	A mold is the shape of a plant or animal left in the sediment when the rock is formed.
3	Wow! That's a lot of information.

All	**And there's still more to discover! [gesture]**
2	But that is all we can uncover today.
3	So until next time, keep digging for information, and we'll see you again soon on...
All	**<u>Fossil Finders!</u> [sound effect—Theme music]**

The Solar System
Curriculum-Based Readers Theatre Script

1   Beep! Beep! Beep!

2   This is a special report from NASA Space Center in Houston, Texas.

3   We have just received communication from Captain Planet and his crew.

4   They have discovered there are 9 planets in the solar system!

5   Solar system? [gesture]

All   **The solar system is made up of the Sun [gesture]**

     The 9 planets

     and their moons

     and other objects that orbit the sun. [gesture] [sound effect]

6   How can you remember all 9 planets?

2   My Very Eager Mother Just Served Us Nine Pizzas.

7   What's that got to do with this?

2   This sentence will help you to remember all 9 planets.

All   **My—the first "M" stands for Mercury.**

8   Mercury is the planet closest to the sun.

All   **My Very**

1   The "V" stands for Venus.

2   Venus is the hottest planet.

All   **My Very Eager**

3   The "E" stands for Earth.

4   Earth is the only planet that can support life—

All   **plants [gesture], animals [sound effect], and people like us!**

9   Keep going!

All   **My Very Eager Mother**

1   The second "M" stands for Mars.

2   Mars is called the red planet—

3   because the soil and rocks are red.

All   **My Very Eager Mother Just**

4   The "J" stands for Jupiter.

1   Jupiter is the largest planet.

All   **My Very Eager Mother Just Served**

2   The "S" stands for Saturn.

3   Saturn has rings.

10   Rings? For fingers, toes or nose?

All   **[gesture] [sound effect]**

4   No! The rings go around the center of the planet.

1   They are made from ice, rocks, and dust.

All   **My Very Eager Mother Just Served Us**

4   "U" stands for Uranus.

1   Uranus is the only planet...

2   that spins on its side. [gesture]

All   **My Very Eager Mother Just Served Us Nine**

3   The "N" stands for Neptune.

11   Neptune has eight moons.

All   **Eight moons! [gesture] [sound effect]**

4   And it's the eighth planet from the sun.

All   **My Very Eager Mother Just Served Us Nine Pizzas!**

12   Pizza! Yum! Yum!

2   The "P" stands for Pluto.

3   Pluto is the smallest planet of all!

4   And the coldest.

All   **[gesture] [sound effect]**

All	**My Very Eager Mother Just Served Us Nine Pizzas!**
13	That sentence is so silly!
1	But, it helps you remember...
All	**All 9 planets in order: Mercury, Venus, Earth, Mars, Jupiter, Saturn, Uranus, Neptune and Pluto!!**
1	Beep! Beep! Beep!
2	Wait! This just in... [gesture]
3	Houston, we have a problem! Scientists have deemed that Pluto is no longer a planet!!
All	**[sound effect] [gesture] But what about our sentence?**
4	Looks like we'll need a new one.
5	Well, we can keep the first words, but...
6	How about Nachos!
7	All you ever think about is food!
6	No! I mean, how about that eager mother serving us nachos instead of nine pizzas!
8	You're brilliant! Got it everybody? Hit it!
All	**My Very Eager Mother Just Served Us Nachos!**
3	Stay tuned for further developments!

Clouds
Curriculum-Based Readers Theatre Script

1   We interrupt this program to bring you a special report about...

All   **Weather conditions.**

2   Here are your channel 320 meteorologists from...

All   **"Weird Weather Wonders!" [sound effect] [gesture]**

3   There's a warm front converging on our location.

4   [sound effect] What's a front?

All   **A front is the boundary [gesture] between air masses of different temperatures [sound effect] [gesture] and humidity. [gesture]**

5   We want to warn our viewers to be on the lookout for four kinds of clouds.

All   **Four kinds of clouds—[gesture]**
Cirrus   [X] [X] [X] [gesture]
Stratus   [X] [X] [X] [gesture]
Cu/mu/lus   [X] [gesture]
Cumulo-nimbus! [X] [X] [X] [gesture]

6   Yes—all these clouds are associated with certain weather conditions.

7   Feathery clouds, for example, are...

All   **cirrus clouds [gesture]**

8   Serious?

All   **Cirrus!**

10   [sound effect—phone ring]

8   Is the caller there?

10   Outside my window, like, uh, I see, like, lots of wispy clouds. Like what could this mean?

11   You are seeing cirrus clouds, which usually mean...

All   **pleasant and fair weather. [gesture]**

9   Now, if you see fluffy white clouds...

12   with flat bottoms,

13   those clouds indicate...

All   **fair weather too. [gesture]**

13   They are known as...

All   **Cumulous clouds. [gesture]**

14   But—when they get larger...

All   **[gesture]**

14   and darker,

All   **[gesture]**

14   they produce...

All   **thunderstorms! [gesture] [sound effect]**

15   And they become...

All   **cumulonimbus clouds!**

16   And our last Weird Wonder Weather kind of cloud...

All   **is...[sound effect] [gesture]**

17   smooth and gray...

18   and covers all of the sky,

All   **blocking out direct sunlight. [gesture]**

4   It often brings light rain and drizzle.

All   **Light rain and drizzle. [gesture]**

12   Is it cirrus?

1   Is it cumulus?

All   **No, it's a stratus cloud! [sound effect]**

3   Uh-oh! Is it a tornado? [gesture]

5   Is it a hurricane? [gesture]

6   Viewers—we are experiencing extreme atmospheric conditions!

7   We will continue to postpone our regularly scheduled program—

All   **Cloudy With a Chance of Meatballs. [gesture]**

Ancient Astronomers
Curriculum-Based Readers Theatre Scripts

1	And now for our program!
All	**[sound effect]**
1	Welcome to a special presentation of...
All	***Smart Dead Guys!* [gesture]**
2	Today's show features...
All	**four ancient astronomers. [gesture]**
3	What's an astronomer?
5	A person who studies the universe and the solar system, or a...
All	**Star-gazer! [gesture] [sound effect]**
6, 7	Our first team of astronomers believed that...
All	**all objects in the solar system revolved around the planet Earth.**
8	Oh—you mean geocentric!
All	**Yes—geo meaning "Earth" and centric meaning "center or middle." [gesture]**
9	So, please welcome...
All	**Aristotle and Ptolemy! [sound effect]**
10	And—from Team Heliocentric—
11	Helio—meaning "sun"...
All	**Ooh—That's hot! [gesture] [sound effect]**
12	and centric meaning, as you know—
All	**"center or middle." [gesture]**
13	So, give it up for...
All	**Copernicus and Galileo [sound effect suggestion: "Galileo, Galileo" as in the song "Bohemian Rhapsody"] [gesture]**
14	...who believed that all objects in the solar system revolved around...
All	**the sun!**
15	Now, from Team Geocentric, please welcome Aristotle.
All	**[gesture] [sound effect]**
16	So, Aristotle, what is your view of the solar system?
17	Let me see... [gesture] I believe that the earth is the center of the universe. Don't you agree?
All	**You mean "geocentric."**
17	Of course that's what I mean. Didn't everyone in the middle ages think that? *[#4 and #26 shake their heads.]*
18	If you're so smart, what else did you believe?
17	All objects in the solar system move in perfect circles around the earth.
All	**Perfect circles around the earth. [gesture]**
17	You do know what a circle is, don't you?
All	**[sound effect]**
18	Thank you, Aristotle. Now let's meet a fellow geocentric thinker—Ptolemy!
19	Tell us Ptolemy when did you live?
20	Well, I was born in 85 AD and died in 165 AD.
All	**Wow! You lived for 80 long years! [sound effect]**
21	What makes you the bees' knees?
20	Well, there are so many things.
21	Maybe it's because you...
All	**wrote a book on the geocentric model. [gesture]**
22	So, like Aristotle, you believed that the earth was the center of the solar system?

20	Yes, yes I did.
23	What makes you different from Aristotle?
20	I had a beard.
All	**A beard? [gesture]**
24	No—that's not it! You believed that...
All	**some planets moved in small circles as they revolved around the Earth.**
18	Thanks, Ptolemy for coming on the show today and sharing your expertise!
25	Next up—some astronomers with different perspectives! Mr. Copernicus—when exactly were you born?
26	In 1473, and I came to an untimely end in 1543.
All	**[sound effect]**
27	Sorry to hear that. We understand you wrote a book about your heliocentric beliefs.
All	**[whispered] Heliocentric—all objects in the solar system revolve around the sun.**
28	What was the name of that book?
26	Ahem, _De revolutionibus orbium coelestium._
All	**Say what? [gesture]**
26	_On the Revolutions of the Heavenly Spheres._
All	**So what was it about?**
26	I'd rather not say. The Church did not agree with me.
2	Why not?

All	**Because the Church accepted <u>geocentric</u> thinking. [gesture]**
26	And they put me in jail!
All	**[gesture] [sound effect]**
3	Sooooo, Mr. Galileo Galilee.
4	You can just call me Galileo.
All	**[sound effect] [gesture]**
5	Why do you agree with Copernicus?
4	My self-made superior vision telescope showed me the way. [gesture]
6	The way?
7	The way out?
All	**The way, way out in the solar system? [gesture]**
4	No—the way the solar system revolved around the sun, and therefore was...
All	**Heliocentric! [gesture] [sound effect]**
8	Thanks for tuning in to...
All	_**Smart Dead Guys!**_ **[gesture]**
9	We'd like to thank our ancient guests, the astronomers...
All	**Aristotle, Ptolemy, Copernicus, and Galileo [gesture] [sound effect]**
10	...for sharing their beliefs about the solar system.
11	Don't forget to tune in next time for _Smart Dead Women._ [gesture]
12	This show was brought to you by Tombstone Ice Cream with its two new flavors—
All	**Heliocentric and Geocentric! [gesture] [sound effect]**
13	Reach for the stars, everyone!

Weather
Curriculum-Based Readers Theatre Script

All   [Rain sound effect]

1   It's raining!

All   Awwww! [gesture]

Rain, rain, go away!

All the children want to play!

1   But we need the rain.

2   Rain makes things grow.

All   [sound effect]

3   Rain comes from the clouds in the sky.

All   [gesture]

4   Clouds are made of water droplets

5   or ice crystals.

6   There are many different kinds of clouds.

All   *[A chant]*

Cir-rus clouds,

Stra-tus clouds,

Cu-mu-lus clouds!

1   And here's a great big cloud name:

All   **Cu-mu-lo-nim-bus!**

2   And now an even bigger name:

All   **Nim-bo-stra-tus!**

3   A fancy name for rain is precipitation.

All   **Precipitation. [gesture]**

4   Precipitation is also snow,

5   freezing rain,

6   ice,

All   and hail! [sound effect] Brrrrr! [gesture]

1   We need some sun!

2   Who knows what the word "temperature" means?

All   **I do! Me! I do! [gesture]**

3   What is it?

All   **Temperature is how hot [gesture] [sound effect]**
or cold [gesture] [sound effect] it is.

4   Right!

5   There are all kinds of weather.

6   There are four seasons of weather.

All   **Four seasons—Winter, spring, summer, and fall.**

1   Some days are sunny.

2   Some days are icy.

3   Some days are partly cloudy.

4   Some days are snow days.

All   **No school! Yay! [gesture]**

5   Some days are foggy.

6   Some days are hot.

All   **Hot! [gesture] [sound effect]**

1   But...

All   **Whether the weather is cold,**
or whether the weather is hot,
we'll weather the weather
whatever the weather,
whether we like it or not! [gesture]

Weather
Curriculum-Based Readers Theatre Script

1   Up next on....

All   **Weird Weather Wonders!**

2   Yes, here on channel 316 is today's weather report.

3   We're going to find out the temperature in _____.

4   What is temperature?

All   **Temperature is the measure of the amount of heat energy [sound effect] in the atmosphere.**

5   Today, temperatures will reach a scorching, cooking 94 degrees.

All   **[gesture] [sound effect]**

6   (female) Hey Billy Bob, what's the air pressure?

7   (male) Well, She-Nay-Nay, air pressure is...

All   **the weight of the air determined by several factors including temperature.**

6   How do you weigh air?

8   To measure air pressure, you use...

All   **A barometer! [gesture]**

9   A thermometer?

All   **No-oh! A Thermometer measures air temperature [gesture] [sound effect]**

10   But...

All   **A barometer measures air pressure. [gesture][sound effect]**

11   Who in the world measures these things?

All   **Meteorologists!**

Boys   Weathermen!

Girls   —or weather <u>women</u>!

12   They also measure wind speed...

All   **[sound effect][gesture]**

13   and precipitation.

All   **[sound effect]**

14   How? What instruments do they use?

All   **[gesture] [sound effect]**

15   Not musical instruments!

All   **Ohhhh!**

16   An anemometer measures wind speed.

All   **Anemometer—Wind speed. [gesture] [sound effect]**

17   You measure precipitation with...

All   **a rain gauge. [gesture][sound effect]**

6   Say, Billy Bob, did you know that the atmospheric conditions create different types of precipitation?

7   Right you are, She-nay-nay! Do you know what causes thunderstorms, hurricanes, and tornadoes?

6   Mm Hmm.

All   **Extreme atmospheric conditions! E.A.C. [gesture]**

10   This report has been brought to you by Subway and its new line of sandwiches:

11   Thunderstorm Turkey,

12   Hurricane Ham, and

18   Tuna Tornado!

14   All served with...

All   **Rain Relish!**

6   This is She-nay-nay...

7   and Billy Bob!

6, 7   Thanks for tuning into...

All   **Weird Weather Wonders! [sound effect] [gesture]**

Reduce, Reuse, and Recycle
Curriculum-Based Readers Theatre Script

1   [sound effect] [gesture] I'm done with this can of soda. [gesture]

All   **[gesture] Stop in the name of Earth! This planet you will hurt. Use it o-o-ver. Use it o-o-ver.**

2   Use it over?

3   How?

All   **Recycle it. [gesture]**

3   Recycle?

All   **Recycle means to reuse. [gesture]**

4   Use paper, plastic, metal, and glass over again.

5   We can use a glass jelly jar as a flower vase.

6   We can use a plastic carton as a planter.

7   An artist can even use old cans to make art.

All   **Use it o-o-ver. Use it o-o-ver. [gesture]**

8   Just think of the dumps we'd put out of business.

9   You said it! Garbage takes up a lot of space and worst of all, it makes our land smell bad.

All   **P.U.! [gesture]**

10   But what's this I hear about a landfill?

All   **A landfill is a place where the garbage is buried so it looks and smells better than a dump. [sound effect]**

10   I like that idea...a place to stash the trash! [gesture] [sound effect]

All   **Stash the trash! [gesture] [sound effect]**

11   But it still doesn't solve the problem of reducing the amount of garbage.

12   Say I hear that word a lot at home. My parents are always talking about reducing.

13   Yeah, reducing—meaning to get smaller. I get it now.

All   **Reduce the amount of garbage. [gesture] [sound effect]**

1   But how?

2   We can buy products that last a long time.

3   Stop buying paper cups that get thrown away once they're used...

All   **...and start thinking jelly jars. [gesture]**

4   Jelly jars? We're recycling them again?

5   You bet. Back to the future!

6   And when people give away old things, it reduces garbage.

5   Give away your tired, old clothes and toys...

All   **...yearning to be reused again and again. [gesture]**

11   My uncle fixes up old cars and resells them. Is that one of the three R's?

12   Three R's? [gesture]

13   The three R's—

All   **Reduce, Reuse, and Recycle! [gesture] [sound effect]**

14   Oh I see—We're talking environmental R's!

15   And they're not just for kids!

16   People all over the U.S. are cutting down on waste because they...

All   **Reduce, reuse, and recycle! [gesture] [sound effect]**

17   In Texas, there's a Trash-off Day!

18   People collect litter from parks, roads, and neighborhoods.

All   **Don't mess with Texas! [gesture] [sound effect]**

19	The people of California had a Clean the Beach Day.	20	Yeah, like on *American Idol*—Let's give back!
20	They picked up all the litter on the beach...	**All**	**Give back! [gesture] [sound effect]**
21	and recycled thousands of metal cans and plastic bottles.	9	Let's spread the word.
22	Their beaches were beautiful again.	1	So the next time I'm done with a can of soda, I'm gonna...
All	**Surfing U.S.A.! [gesture] [sound effect]**	**All**	**[gesture] Stop in the name of Earth! This planet you will hurt. Use it o-o-ver. Use it o-o-ver.**
7	What can we do here at our school...	10	Because everyone can...
8	to give back or get back a cleaner place to learn and play?	**All**	**Reduce, Reuse, and Recycle! [gesture] [sound effect]**

The Eight Geographical Regions of North America
Curriculum-Based Readers Theatre Script

1   Please fasten your seat belts.

All   **[gesture] [sound effect]**

2   Welcome aboard your aerial tour.

All   **The Fabulous Futuristic Flying Textbook! [gesture] [sound effect]**

1   Where our motto is...

All   **See the whole U.S.A. in just one day!**

3   Today we will be sightseeing!

4   Flying over...

All   **The 8 geographical regions of North America! [gesture] [sound effect]**

5   Our first location or region has great harbors....

6   broad lowlands, and it is next to large bodies of water.

7   You mean like Sea World?

All   **No! The Coastal Plains!**

8   That was so much fun! Where are we going next?

9   Lets soar west to the Appalachian Mountains.

10   Check out those old eroded mountains.

All   **[sound effect] [gesture]**

11   Our next location is a giant horseshoe....

12   Whoa—that must be one big horse! [sound effect]

11   Let me finish! I meant the land that's wrapped around the Hudson Bay!

All   **The Canadian Shield, eh?**

13   Hey look pal—see all those glaciers

14   I know, right?

13   Those glaciers probably carved those lakes...

14   and those rock formations.

15   Our next location is the Interior Lowlands.

All   **The Interior Lowlands. [gesture] [sound effect]**

16   Hey man, I hope you brought your canoes because this place is full of...

All   **rolling flat lands, rivers, and valleys...**

17   and grassy hills.

18   I hope we see some buffaloes.

19   So, what's next?

20   Well, what's great and what's plain?

19   I don't know. Your dog?

20   No—it's...

All   **The Great Plains! [gesture] [sound effect]**

21   Is that the place that has a lot of buffalo and flat, boring land?

All   **Yes! Go west where the skies are blue! Go west! This is what we're gonna do!**

22   And it also has an increase of elevation—

All   **westward. [gesture]**

23   Right. And grassy lands.

24   Okay, so—The Great Plains have...

All   **buffalo, an increase of elevations, and grassy lands that are flat. [gesture]**

25   What's that?

All   **Flat! [gesture]**

1   Our next region is...

2   Drum roll please!

All   **[sound effect]**

3   The Rocky Mountains!

4   Whaa?

All   **The Rocky Mountains!**

 Developed by Rosalind M. Flynn ★ www.rosalindflynn.com

4	I'm scared of those high, rugged mountains!
1	May Day! May Day!
5	Not funny. I'm scared of that Continental Divide.
6	No need to be afraid, The Continental Divide is simply and imaginary line.
Right Half of Group	East of the line, water flows to the Atlantic. [gesture]
Left Half of Group	West of the line, water flows to the Pacific. [gesture]
7	Our next geographical region is the Basin.
8	No, it's the Basin Range.
All	**Stop! [gesture] It's the Basin and Range.**
9	Yes, we are now west of the Rocky Mountains...
10	and east of the Sierra Nevada and the Cascades.
11	See the isolated mountains...
12	and Death Valley.
All	**[sound effect] Death Valley—the lowest point in North America! [gesture]**
13	Where are we going next?
14	Flying further west—we're now along the Pacific Coast.
15	See the mountains and fertile valleys!
All	**Ohhh, we love the Coastal Range. It's so magical! [gesture]**
16	Thank you for soaring with...
All	**The Fabulous Futuristic Flying Textbook. [gesture] [sound effect]**
17	Who said learning can't be fun?
18	As we begin our descent into the Coastal Range...
19	Please make sure your seatbelts and tray tables are in the...
All	**upright and locked positions. [gesture] [sound effect]**
20	And if you don't want to fail Earth Science, remember the following—
All	**[chant]**
	Eight [X] [X]
	Eight regions [X]
	Eight regions in the [X]
	Norte, Norte, Norte **[X]**
	of America.
All	**One—[X] Coastal Plains.**
	Two—[X] Appalachian Mountains.
	Three—[X] Canadian Shield, Shield, Shield, Shield.
	Four—[X] Interior Lowlands.
	Five—[X] Great Plains.
	Six—[X] The Really Rocky Mountains.
	Seven—[X] Basin and Range.
	And the last one is [X] Coastal Range!

Cells
Curriculum-Based Readers Theatre Script

1   Good morning, travelers!

2   Thank you for booking a tour with...

All   Mighty Micro Tours... [sound effect]

3   where our motto is...

All   "We CELL-abrate the basic unit of life!" [gesture]

4   Today's destination is...

All   An animal cell! [sound effect]

5   Our tour through this building block of all organisms will include...

6   three important stops—

7   The cell membrane,

All   The skin! [gesture]

8   The cytoplasm,

All   The goo! [gesture]

9   ...and the nucleus.

All   The brain! [gesture]

10   Our first stop today is the cell membrane.

All   The skin! [gesture]

10   This fluid-like layer is composed—

All   —"made up"— [gesture]

10   ...of proteins and carbs.

11   Oh, I get it! The cell membrane protects the cell.

All   Yeah! The cell membrane protects the cell! [gesture]

11   The cell membrane decides what gets in and what gets out of the cell.

10   Brace yourselves for impact.

All   [gesture]

10   We're going in!

All   [sound effect] [gesture]

12   Wow! What a rush!

11-13   What is that stuff? [gesture]

10   That jelly-like substance is cytoplasm! [gesture]

All   The goo! [gesture]

10   The cytoplasm protects the cell organelles.

All   Protects and serves! [gesture]

14   Brace yourselves. We are about to enter through the double membrane of the largest organelle in the animal cell.

All   The nucleus—a.k.a—

15   The brain!

16   The boss!

14   The control center!

15   The drill sergeant who commands reproduction and cell metabolism.

All   Nucleus—Sir, Yes sir! [gesture]

17   Nucleus characteristics: Repeat after me. Round.

All   Round. [gesture]

17   Dark.

All   Dark. [gesture]

17   Large and in charge.

All   Large and in charge. [gesture]

14   Oh, look—something shiny in the nucleus.

All   [gesture]

15   What's that?

17   Those are special strands of genetic info called chromosomes.

16   Is that like DNA?

17   That's classified information.

All   [gesture] Shh! Classified genetic information.

18   As we wade leave the nucleus,

All   The brain! [sound effect]

18   We meet—

19-23   The Organelles! Do-wop-shooby do! Do-wop-shooby do! [gesture]

18   There are six members of this group—

19-23   The Organelles! Do-wop-shooby do! Do-wop-shooby do! [gesture]

19   Please step into the first one—The E.R.

20   The E.R.—Is somebody sick?

All   No! E.R. stands for Endoplasmic Reticulum.

21   The E.R. is a network of canals...

22   filled with fluid.

23   You mean like a transport system?

All   Yes!

18   Let's continue our tour. Onto the next organelle.

All   [gesture] [sound effect] Warp speed ahead!

24   Now that we are in the cytoplasm,

25   if you will look to your left, you will see the...

All: Ribsomes Factory, Yeah!

26   They have been busy producing proteins for years.

All   [sound effect] [gesture] Ribsomes produce proteins.

24   Watch your step!

All   [gesture]

25   There is rough endoplasmic reticulum below—lining the membranes.

All   Endoplasmic Reticulum, yuck! [gesture]

26   Oooh!!! Is that pancakes I see?

ALL: Mmmm! [gesture]

24   No, those flattened membranous stacks are Golgi bodies storing protein until...

ALL: it leaves the cell. Out of here! [gesture]

1   Now, if everyone will kindly shift your attention to the right [gesture], we are coming upon the lysosome.

2   Lysol?

All   No—lysosome!

3   Lysosomes are small, sac-like structures surrounded by a single membrane.

2   What's in the bag?

All   It's a sac—not a bag!

4   This sac contains strong digestive enzymes.

1   Not only that, but when released, the enzymes can break down worn-out organelles or food.

All   Break it down! Break it down! [gesture]

2   I heard a rumor that lysosomes are also referred to as "suicide sacs!"

All   [gesture] [sound effect]

3   Now, don't be afraid—lysosomes just break down worn-out cell parts.

All   [gesture] [sound effect]

5   Continuing on, we see the mitochondria. [gesture]

All   Check out all that POWER! Ooooh!

6   I may look like a tube, but I'm the powerhouse. [gesture] I'm really into respiration. [sound effect]

All   What is respiration? [sound effect]

7   Respiration is the releasing of food energy from food molecules that are used by the cell.

All	**All cells have mitochondria, but muscle cells have more! [sound effect] TO PUMP YOU UP! [gesture]**
8	We have now arrived at our final destination.
All	**The Rest Stop of the Cell! [sound effect] The vacuoles!**
9	Look—I see the snack machine!
7	That's because vacuoles store food, water, sugar, and minerals.
8	I see restrooms!
All	**[sound effect]**
9	That's because they store waste products here.
All	**Waste products! Ewww!**
7	It sounds like they're cleaning, too. Listen.
All	**[gesture] [sound effect]**
8	You hear that because vacuoles act as a vacuum to clean the cell.
All	**[sound effect]**
9	It is clean in here!
1	And that concludes today's tour with...
All	**Mighty Micro Tours... [sound effect]**
3	where our motto is...
All	**"We CELL-abrate the basic unit of life!" [gesture]**

Mammals
Curriculum-Based Readers Theatre Script

1   Welcome to Animal Boot Camp!

All   Yes, sir! [gesture]

1   I am Officer Bear, your mammal sergeant.

All   Yes, sir! [gesture]

1   These are my cadets,

2   Ricky Raccoon,

3   Donna Dog, and...

4   Herbert Horse.

2   For the next month, you will learn about classifying animals.

3   Classifying animals!

All   Classifying animals?

4   What's that? [gesture]

1   When you classify, you put animals that are alike in some ways...

2   into the same group.

3   This week's group—Mammals!

All   Yes sir, mammals, sir! [gesture]

1   First, you need animals with fur or hair. [gesture]

2   What comes first?

All   Animals with fur or hair, sir!

2   Right! Fur or hair is one characteristic of a mammal!

3   Next, you need an animal born alive.

All   Not in an egg, sir?

4   No! Most mammals are born alive.

All   Mammals—born alive, sir. [gesture]

1   Also, mammal babies drink their mama's milk.

All   Mammals—mama's milk—yes, sir!

2   Any questions?

All   Do all mammals live on land, sir?

3   No! Whales and dolphins are mammals that live in the ocean.

All   Thank you, sir, for keeping us straight. [gesture]

1   I don't know what you have heard. (marching in place)

All   (echo) I don't know what you have heard. (marching in place)

1   Mammals all have hair or fur.

All   Mammals all have hair or fur.

1   Mammal babes are born alive.

All   Mammal babes are born alive.

1   They need their mama's milk to thrive.

All   They need their mama's milk to thrive.

1   Sound off!

All   Hair or fur!

1   Sound off!

All   Born alive!

1   Sound off!

All   Mama's milk!

Sound off 1, 2—Mammals! [gesture]

Butterflies
Curriculum-Based Readers Theatre Script

1   They drink nectar!

2   They love the spring

3   They are totally symmetrical.

4   They flutter each wing. [gesture]

5   They are...

All   Beautiful, Brilliant, Blushing Butterflies! [gesture] [sound effect]

6   Hi! We are your hosts for tonight's dazzling show!

7   We are your lepidopterists!

8   What is a lepidopterist?

All   A lepidopterist is someone who studies beautiful, brilliant, blushing, butterflies! [gesture]

9   How many body parts does a butterfly have?

**All   Three. [X] Three body parts.
Head, thorax, abdomen, abdomen [gesture]
Head, thorax, abdomen, abdomen [gesture]**

10   Ew! What's that long straw thing coming out of the butterfly's mouth?

11   That's its tongue!

All   [sound effect] The Scientific Terminology is proboscis.

12   Wha... Wha... What's that butterfly doing on that flower?

All   Chill out!

13   The butterfly is just...

All   chilling out – basking its wings in the sun. [gesture] [sound effect]

14   Look at those cool patterns on the delicate wings.

All   [sound effect] By our account, the wing colors help butterflies with camouflage, mating, and mimicry!

15   Camouflage – blending into the environment!

16   Mating – helping the male and female find each other.

17   Mimicry – looking like something else in nature.

18   Well I guess we've learned everything about butterflies!

All   Not quite!

19   Then what did we leave out?

**All   Butterflies – they love to feel with their feet!
Butterflies – Two antennae – sweet!
Legs, legs – skinny legs!
Eggs, eggs – they start as eggs!
Next stage is the pupa stage—**

20   What's the pupa stage?

All   Pupa is a caterpillar! Followed by chrysalis!

21   Chrysalis?

All   Chrysalis – that's where all the magic happens! [gesture]

22   What magic?

All   The transformation into an adult Beautiful, Brilliant, Blushing Butterfly! [gesture] [sound effect]

The Six Kingdoms of Life
Curriculum-Based Readers Theatre Script

1   [sound effect]

2   Hello, Welcome to the...

All   Homework Hotline. [sound effect]

3   1-800 - H-O-M-E-W-O-R-K...

4   where students get lots of help with their...

All   Hard Homework! [sound effect] [gesture]

5   Press 1 for Math.

6   Press 2 for Social Studies.

7   Press 3 for Science.

8   [sound effect]

9   You have selected Science.

10   Please hold for your Homework Hotline Helpers!

11   [sound effect] Homework Hotline!

12   My friends and I are really bombing Science! We have a test on the Kingdoms of Life tomorrow.

11   Please hold while I get the Science experts.

ALL   We'll try the Science Guys! [X]
We'll try the Science Guys! [X]
Will, Will, [X] Will, Will, Will!
We'll try the Science Guys. [X]
Science Rules! [gesture]

8   [sound effect] You have reached your homework Hotline Science experts.

13   First of all, the kingdoms of life, who even knows what they are?

14   Yeah, what's up with the kingdoms of life?

ALL   The kingdoms of life are a way to classify all living organisms.

15   Does that include my pesky brother?

All   Unfortunately, yes! [gesture]

16   Can you please just name them?

All   Archaebacteria, Eubacteria, Protista, Fungi, Plantae and Animalia. [sound effect]

17   Did you name six kingdoms? I thought there were only five?

8   Actually, the Moneran kingdom recently split into two because of its enormous size.

18   Archaebacteria and Eubacteria, what's the DIF?

All   Archaebacteria is bacteria that has no nucleus [gesture] and lives in extreme environments.

13   Like geothermal vents and acid pits?

All   Precisely! [gesture]

19   Sorry, I am late; I had to take my penicillin.

1   Lad, did you know that penicillin is a type of Eubacteria?

13-19   Eubacteria?

All   Like Archaebacteria, Eubacteria has no nucleus, but does not live in extreme environments.

19   Do you mean I just swallowed bacteria?

All   Indeed, but you swallowed good bacteria, not harmful bacteria like E. Coli. [sound effect]

13   Okay, I understand. Tell us more about the rest of the kingdoms, starting with Protista.

2   Protista are usually single-celled organisms and they have a nucleus.

14   Any more facts?

3	Most organisms in the Protista kingdom can only be seen through a microscope.
4	However, slime molds and algae can be seen with the naked eye.
All	**Protista: usually single-celled, have a nucleus, can be seen through microscopes, look like slimy mold with naked eye. [gesture]**
15	What's Fungi? I never understood that kingdom!
16	Yeah my mom is a baker and she told me that fungi helps her make bread, but never told me how!
5	Your mom is right. Yeast is an example of fungi which helps bread rise. Fungi are also multi-cellular. They steal food from decaying matter without being able to move.
15	Aren't mushrooms a type of fungi? My brother ate a mushroom and got sick.
17	Hey my brother is a FUN GUY, but he never steals food.
6	No, we are not talking about fun people; we are talking about a kingdom of life.
All	**Fun statements about Fungi are that they are multi-cellular, steal food from decaying matter, and can steal food even though they can't move! [gesture]**
18	Wait, aren't mushrooms a part of the plant kingdom? What's the DIF?
7	First of all, Plantae make their own food and mushrooms don't, so...
All	**mushrooms are in the Fungi kingdom.**
19	Yeah that's right, I remember my teacher talking about chlorophyll and photosynthesis, but I don't know what they are.
13	I think you were goofing off in class.
All	**Photosynthesis is the process where the plant converts the sun's energy using chlorophyll into oxygen and food. [sound effect]**
16	What kingdom do we human beings fall into?
8	Funny you should ask. We are part of the Animalia kingdom.
15	Let me guess. Unfortunately, my pesky brother is part of the Animalia kingdom too?
9	Yes, he is a mammal just like you. He is also multi-cellular, consumes living things for energy, and, like most Animalia, he can move.
17	My teacher was just talking about examples of Animalia yesterday.
18	I think he said insects, reptiles, crustaceans, mammals and fish as some examples.
All	**Animalia: multicellular, consume food, and move. [gesture]**
13-19	Wow that's a lot of information.
19	I hear my mom calling me for dinner. I think we're having meatloaf.
10	Did you know that meatloaf is...
13-19	Gotta go bye.
10	Thank you for calling...
All	**Homework Hotline [sound effect]**
3	1-800 - H-O-M-E-W-O-R-K
4	...where students get lots of help with their...
All	**Hard Homework! [gesture] [sound effect]**

Electricity
Curriculum-Based Readers Theatre Script

1   Ladies and gentlemen, boys and girls, let us introduce you to...

All   **[sound effect] Electricity!**

2   What's electricity?

All   **Electricity is a form of energy and light. [gesture]**

3   Don't you people know anything?

4   Do we have electricity inside of <u>us</u>?

5   No, we have <u>energy</u> inside us...

6   which makes us walk, run, throw a ball, and sometimes even...

All   **clean our rooms! [gesture]**

7   That's work!

8   Yo! You know electrical energy also does work.

9   It lights your house.

10   Electrical energy also brings you sound for your iPod.

11   (singing) Oh yeah!

12   Get over it! Let's get back on the subject. Electricity also cools your house.

11   My house is already cool.

12   No, I mean air conditioning!

13   *Your* energy comes from your food.

1   But for lights and stuff, the electricity has to be made.

2   You go girl!

3   Electrical wires are made up of tiny atoms.

4   What is an atom?

5   You mean like in math when you add 'em up?

4   No, *atom*, spelled A-T-O-M.

All   **Atoms are tiny bits or particles and each atom has smaller particles. [gesture]**

5   Oh. Now I get it.

6   Hey, look over there. It's a generator.

All   **[gesture—All look where 6 points.]**

7   Is that a magnet inside some coils?

8   Yes, the generator spins a magnet inside the coils.

9   And there are even <u>bigger</u> generators than this one.

All   **Awesome! [gesture]**

10   Big generators need much more power to spin their coils or magnets.

11   Where does that power come from?

12   Wind, **[sound effect]**

13   flowing water, **[sound effect]**

1   or steam. **[sound effect]**

All   **Wind, flowing water, or steam produce power! [gesture]**

2   As the coils or magnets spin, electricity flows in the coils.

7   The electricity flows for many miles.

8   How?

All   **Through wires that bring the electricity to homes, schools, stores, and so forth.**

9   And then to your telephones, clocks, TVs, stoves, computers, and....well, you get it.

All   **Right. We got it all—**
[chant]
Energy, atoms, generators, [X]
Coils, magnets, wires! [X]—
Electricity is powerful stuff!
[sound effect] [gesture]

Sound
Curriculum-Based Readers Theatre Script

1   Greetings Earthlings!

2   We bring you signs of peace from the planet U.B. Mute...

3   where there is no sound.

4   We need to bring back all data on sound so that we Mutons...

1-4   can communicate with you Earthlings.

All   **Sounds like we can help you!**

1   What is sound anyway?

All   **Sound is a form of energy made by vibrating molecules. [sound effect] [gesture]**

1-4   Vibrating molecules. [sound effect] [gesture]

5   Hey Mutons, here's another sound factoid—

All   **Sound is created by matter striking matter!**

   [gesture—Stomp, stomp, slap] "Uh!"

1-4   [gesture—Stomp, stomp, slap] "Uh!"

6   That "Uh" has a low pitch!

1-4   Pitch? What is this pitch you speak of?

All   **Pitch is the highness [gesture] or the lowness [gesture] of a sound.**

7, 8   Repeat after us!

7   High pitch—fast frequency!

All   **High pitch—Fast frequency!**

8   Low Pitch—Slow frequency!

All   **Low Pitch—Slow Frequency!**

1   What is frequency?

All   **Frequency is how many wavelengths go by [gesture] in a certain amount of time. [sound effect] [gesture]**

1-4   Sounds like a plan!

9   But wait! There's more!

10   You Mutons—

All   **M-Dogs! [gesture]**

10   ...still need to know about...

All   **Wavelengths, compressions, and rarefactions too! [X]**
   This is more data from us to you! [X] [gesture]

11   Ready everyone?

All   **Wavelength [gesture] is the distance between two compressions or rarefactions.**

1-4   Compression? Rarefaction?

12   A compression is the part of the compressional wave where the molecules are...

All   **tightly packed!**
   [gesture] [sound effect]

3   What if the molecules are...

1-4   far apart? [gesture]

13   That my dear M-Dogs is...

All   **Rarefaction. [gesture]**

1-4   Will sound travel through space?

All   **NO WAY! [gesture] [chant]**
   Sound travels.... [X]
   worst through a gas. [X]
   Going through a liquid— second easiest to pass. [X]
   But sound through a solid goes fast! fast! fast! [gesture]

4   We M-Dogs thank you....

1   We will soon return to your planet to hear more about....

1-4   All Forms of Life!

All   **Sounds GREAT! [Sound Effect: Hum space-age theme music.]**

Saturated Solutions
Curriculum-Based Readers Theatre Script

1	Want some Kool Aid?
2	Sure. Just mix that powder with the water.
1	[gesture] [sound effect]
Evens	**What's all that nasty stuff on the bottom of the pitcher? [sound effect]**
3	Pardon me, but your solution is obviously saturated.
Evens	**Huh? English please!**
5	A solution is composed of a solute that has dissolved into a solvent.
Evens	**Solution? Solute? Solvent? [gesture]**
4	What in the world are they?
7	When a solid dissolves into a liquid, it's called a solution.
6	Oh I get it, like the ocean.
8	Or iced tea.
Evens	**Or like our Kool Aid! [gesture]**
5	Exactly!
Odds	**Precisely. [gesture]**
10	Then, what's a solute?
9	A solute is another word for a solid in a solution.
12	Oh I get it, like the salt in the ocean water,
14	or sugar in your ice tea,
Evens	**or our Kool Aid powder!**
11	So I suppose you don't know what a solvent is either?
14	Is she that new rapper?
13	Not even close.
Odds	**A solvent is the liquid part of a solution.**

14	Oh! [gesture]
15	Average minds are so slow.
Odds	**Umm hmmm...We agree!**
16	Hey! We're smart in our own special way!
18	Yeah we get it.
Evens	**A solvent is like the water in the ocean.**
20	Or the water in iced tea.
Evens	**Or the water in our Kool Aid!**
2	Uh, okay, but why is all that nasty stuff still at the bottom of the pitcher? [gesture]
3	Like I said before—
Odds	**Your solution is saturated! [gesture]**
22	Solution, I remember. It's when a solid dissolves into a liquid. But why is it saturated?
21	It's saturated because no more solute can dissolve in the solvent.
Evens	**It can't take anymore! [gesture]**
4	I can't take much more of this in general.
6	So the water in the Kool Aid is so full it can't take any more Kool Aid powder?
7	Exactly.
Odds	**Precisely. [gesture]**
8	So what do we do now?
9	I believe it's time for a review.
Evens	**Do we have to?**
Odds	**If you want your Kool Aid!**
11	Define "solution!"

Evens	Solution – when a solid disappears in to a liquid.
Odds	Correct! [gesture]
13	Define "solute."
Evens	Solute – the solid in a solution.
Odds	A-okay. [gesture]
15	Define "solvent."
Evens	Solvent – the liquid in a solution.
Odds	Absolutely! [gesture]
17	Define "saturated."
Evens	Saturated – when a solution can't absorb any more of the solid. It's full!
Odds	You got it! [gesture]
All	Time for Kool Aid! [gesture]
10	It probably won't taste good with so much powder added.
12	Saturated or not, I'm thirsty!
Evens	Me, too! [gesture]
Odds	22 glasses of saturated solution coming up! [gesture]
All	[gesture] [sound effect]

Matter
Curriculum-Based Readers Theatre Script

1   Ladies and gentlemen!

2   Boys and girls!

3   Welcome to tonight's program...

All   **"Matter Matters!"**
[gesture] [sound effect]

4   What's matter?

5   My pet monkey Fitzgerald ran away!

6   Not What's <u>the</u> matter – What's matter?

ALL   **Matter is anything that takes up space [gesture] and has mass. [gesture] [sound effect]**

7   Like a tree or like a cup of tea. [gesture]

All   **Or like me! [gesture]**

8   Tonight's show,

All   **"Matter Matters," [gesture] [sound effect]**

8   is brought to you by...

All   **zillions of molecules! [gesture]**

9   Molecules that are always in motion!

10   Starring in tonight's show are...

All   **The 3 types of matter [gesture]**

11   From the Solid State here's Sammy Solid!

All   **One Smart Solid!**
[gesture] [sound effect]

4   He's in such great shape!

12   From the Liquid State, please welcome Lily Liquid!

All   **She just goes with the flow. [gesture] [sound effect]**

13   From the Gas State, we hope you enjoy Gary Gas!

All   **He's one floating, free spirit! [gesture] [sound effect]**

14   Can you tell us about yourself, Sammy Solid?

15   I keep in shape and all my molecules are tightly packed. [gesture]

All   **Tightly packed. [gesture]**

16   Now, splashy Lily Liquid, can you tell us about yourself?

17   I don't care what shape I'm in! I change my shape to fit the latest fashion in containers!

All   **You flow girl! [gesture]**

18   Gary Gas, you smell good today.

19   Thank you. Thank you very much.

18   Tell us – Why don't you keep your shape?

19   My job is to fill the space and let my molecules float freely!

All   **Free at last! [gesture]**

1   Sorry folks, but it's time now to say good-bye to...

All   **Solid, Liquid, and Gas: The 3 types— or states—of matter! [gesture]**

2   Join us next time when we'll talk about...

3   physical and chemical changes!

5   Here on...

All   **"Matter Matters!"**
[gesture] [sound effect]

Atoms
Curriculum-Based Readers Theatre Script

1   Three, two, one – we're live!

2   Up next on...

All   **iAdam! [sound effect]**

3   ...we'll take an intriguing look into the world of...

All   **Atoms! [sound effect] [gesture]**

4   So give it up for that guy known as the building block of all matter—

2   so small that, actually, he cannot be seen by the human eye—

4   Our host –

All   **Adam the Atom! [gesture] [sound effect]**

5   Good evening, science fans! It is I—Adam the Atom!

All   **"Atom" from the Greek meaning un-cuttable or indivisible! [gesture]**

6   Hey Adam—show us what you're made of!

5   Ha ha! Of course! I am the smallest unit of an element, but a big part of me is here with us tonight!

7   Ladies and gentlemen, please welcome...

8   The man full of protons and neutrons—

9   Who's the man?

All   **Nuke the Nucleus! [gesture] [sound effect]**

11   I just love being the center of attention.

12   That's because he's the center of the atom.

13   Can I have your autograph?

14   I'm your biggest fan!

15   Hey—what's that cloud of negativity surrounding the Nuke the Nucleus?

5   Fans, it's none other than that whiz kid who runs circles around my nucleus—

All   **Electronica Electron! [gesture]**

16   Watch out—I am negatively charged today.

17   Aren't electrons always negatively charged?

18   Shh! Yes, but let's not get on her bad side.

19   What about your protons and neutrons, Adam?

20   Yeah—don't we get to meet them tonight?

All   **Protons! Neutrons! Protons! Neutrons! [gesture]**

11   Adam—since I am made up of protons and neutrons, please let me do the honor.

5   Go right ahead, Nuke!

11   By popular demand, right here on iAdam, those two parts of an atom that have the most atomic weight—Protons....

All   **Protons with their positive electrical charge? [gesture]**

11   Positively! And—Neutrons....

All   **Those no charge/neutral Neutrons? [gesture]**

11   Absolutely! Here they are!

21,22   Hi everyone. We're proud to join forces with Electronica Electron and be called...

16,21,22   The three basic parts of an atom!

All   **Protons! Neutrons! Electrons! [gesture]**

5   I can't tell you how emotional I'm feeling to have all of you on my show!

All   **[sound effect]**

5	You're part of me—Adam the Atom—and you always will be!
2	Adam, we're just about out of time now.
3	But there's more to know about the intriguing world of...
All	**Atoms! [sound effect] [gesture]**
4	There certainly is!
6	Join us for next week's show and you'll learn why atoms bond!
All	**[sound effect]**

7	Let's thank that guy known as the building block of all matter—
8	—so small that actually, he cannot be seen by the human eye—
9	Our host –
All	**Adam the Atom!** **[gesture] [sound effect]**
10	And we'll see all you science fans right here next week on...
All	**iAdam! [sound effect]**

Magnets
Curriculum-Based Readers Theatre Script

1   Attract [gesture]—Repel [gesture]

All   **Attract [gesture]—Repel [gesture]**

        Attract [gesture]—Repel [gesture]

2   Excuse me. Could somebody tell us what's going on here?

3   Um, yeah. I mean, like, what's happening?

4   And why are you all going....

All   **Attract [gesture]—Repel [gesture]**

        Attract [gesture]—Repel [gesture]

5   We're just a bunch of magnets.

2, 3, 4   Magnets?

All   **Yeah, magnets— things that attract other magnets. [gesture]**

6   We're just trying to get in shape. Magnetic Field Day is next week!

2, 3, 4   Attract [gesture]—Repel? [gesture]

        Attract [gesture]—Repel? [gesture]

All   **Attract [gesture], in fact, just means to pull together. [gesture]**

        Repel [gesture], oh well, just means to push apart. [gesture]

2   Why do you want to get in shape?

7   We have got to be able to attract other magnets.

8   Right! We magnets need to shape up our iron, nickel, and other metals!

All   **Iron, nickel, and other metals—that's some of the material we're made of!**

3   And just where will all of this happen?

9   In a magnetic field, of course!

2,3,4   What's a magnetic field?

10   Don't these kids know anything? [gesture]

All   **A magnetic field is the invisible area around us magnets that carries magnetic force to other objects. [gesture]**

2,3,4   Oh. Sounds powerful.

All   **Uh huh. That's right—'cause we've got magnetic force—the push or pull of a magnet! [gesture] [sound effect]**

11   Magnetism is one of the main forces of nature, kids.

4   Like gravity?

All   **Yes, like gravity—which causes objects to be attracted to each other. [gesture]**

12, 13   Magnetism, on the other hand,

All   **causes <u>magnetized</u> objects to be attracted to each other. [gesture]**

2,3,4   Oh yeah, we see. [gesture] [sound effect]

12, 13   Oh no you do not see! [gesture] [sound effect]

14   No one can actually see magnetism.

All   **Magnetism is an invisible force that can make some things move towards each other, [gesture]**

15   move away from each other, [gesture]

All   **or stay in one place. [gesture] [sound effect]**

2   Invisible? Then how do you know it's real?

16   Even though you can't see magnetism,

All   **you can look at magnets and see what happens to things that are put near them. [gesture] [sound effect]**

17	When magnets and some metals are inside a magnetic field, magnetism makes them move.	**All**	**a magnet created by passing an electric current through coils of wire. [gesture] [sound effect]**
18	Back to our workout, magnets!	4	What's a...? [gesture]
3	Wait a minute! One more magnet question—What's an electromagnet?	17	No more questions! We've got to be attractive for Magnetic Field Day.
16	An electromagnet is...	**All**	**Attract [gesture]—Repel [gesture]**
			Attract [gesture]—Repel [gesture]

Science Fair Projects
Curriculum-Based Readers Theatre Script

1	Welcome to Science Fair Boot Camp!
All	**Yes, sir!**
1	I am Officer Ray, your Science Fair sergeant.
All	**Yes, sir!**
1	These are my cadets, Jones, Johnson, and James. [Played by Speakers 2, 3, and 4]
2	For the next two weeks, you will learn how to do your Science Fair project.
1	First, you need a science problem.
2	What comes first?
All	**The science problem, sir!**
2	Right! The scientific problem to be solved!
3	Next, you must make an educated guess about your outcome!
4	What is this educated guess called?
All	**Hypothesis, sir!**
4	Hypothesis! Correct!
3	You also need materials!
4	In a List!
All	**Materials List! Check!**
1	Who knows what comes next?
5	Conclusion!
1	Wrong! Drop and give me 5!
6	[Laughs at 5]
2	You think it's funny?
6	Uhhhh...
2	Drop and give me 5!
3	The accurate answer is
All	**Procedures, sir!**
1	Correct! The steps in your project!

All	**[marching]** **Step by Step! Step by Step!**
4	Halt! [Pause for marching to stop.] Following procedures, you need...?
7	Design, sir!
4	Excellent, Private!
1	And what does design mean?
All	**Design is format! [gesture]**
8	It's the way you investigate your problem, sir!
1	Correct!
2	And is that all you need in a Science Fair project?
All	**No, sir! [gesture]**
3	What else is there?
9	Results, sir!
10	Conclusions!
All	**[marching]** **Results! Conclusions!** **Results! Conclusions!**
3	Halt! [Pause for marching to stop.] Meaning?
9	Results tell what happened in your experiment.
10	Conclusions discuss what you learned, sir!
4	All right, soldiers. Drill time! Science Fair Projects! Hut 2, 3, 4!
All	**[marching]** **Question, 2, 3, 4!** **Hypothesis, 2, 3, 4!** **Materials, 2, 3, 4!** **Procedures, 2, 3, 4!** **Design, 2, 3, 4!** **Results, 2, 3, 4!** **Conclusions, 2, 3, 4!**

1   Halt! [Pause for marching to stop.]

Attention!

You're a scruffy looking group, but we'll shape you up here at Science Fair Boot Camp!

All   **Sir! Yes, sir! [gesture]**

2   Dismissed!

Developed by Rosalind M. Flynn ★ www.rosalindflynn.com

Also by Rosalind M. Flynn

DRAMATIZING THE CONTENT WITH CURRICULUM-BASED READERS THEATRE, GRADES 6-12

This book details the process of writing, revising, rehearsing, performing, and assessing original readers theatre scripts based on curriculum content. Even though the title identifies the book as being focused on grades 6-12, **the process described has been used with students as young as grade 2.**

A DRAMATIC APPROACH TO READING COMPREHENSION: *Strategies and Activities for Classroom Teachers*

Rosalind and co author Lenore Blank Kelner designed this book on four drama strategies—Story Dramatization, Character Interviews, Tableau, and Human Slide Shows—for teachers with limited experience in drama. Readers will find detailed explanations of how to lead effective educational drama experiences that increase reading comprehension.

Visit Rosalind's web site for information about her books and the professional development courses, workshops, and summer institutes that she presents.

www.rosalindflynn.com

Rosalind also offers online presentations about her Curriculum-Based Readers Theatre work. Complete information can be found at this web site.

www.ArtsEducationOnline.org

Made in the USA
Middletown, DE
14 November 2019